THE OTHER AMERICA

DR.
MARTIN
LUTHER
KING JR.

————

THE OTHER
AMERICA

**MartinLuther
KingJr.** *Library*

MartinLuther
KingJr.*Library*

"The Other America" reprinted by arrangement with the Estate of Martin Luther King, Jr., Inc., c/o Writers House as the proprietor, New York, N.Y. Copyright © 1967 Dr. Martin Luther King Jr. © renewed 1991 Coretta Scott King.

Foreword Copyright © 2026 by Martin Luther King III

In Association With **IPM**
INTELLECTUAL PROPERTIES
MANAGEMENT, INC.

License granted by Intellectual Properties Management, Inc., Atlanta, GA, exclusive licensor of The King Estate.

HarperCollins books may be purchased for educational, business, or sales promotional use. For information, please email the Special Markets Department at SPsales@harpercollins.com.

hc.com

Designed by Jason Kayser
Art © jakkapan/stock.adobe.com

Library of Congress Cataloging-in-Publication Data has been applied for.

ISBN 978-0-06-346904-4

Printed in the United States of America

26 27 28 29 30 LBC 5 4 3 2 1

Foreword

By Martin Luther King III

On April 14, 1967, less than a year before he was assassinated, my father, Martin Luther King Jr., delivered his speech "The Other America" at Stanford University. Ten days earlier, he had delivered a speech about the damage he felt the war in Vietnam was doing to our country, which had gotten a lot of attention worldwide. He believed that US involvement in the Vietnam War was draining resources that could be used to expand economic opportunities for all in America.

But he felt that it was also important to keep a strong focus on the struggle for civil and human rights in America, and so he was glad to accept the invitation to speak at Stanford about the tragedies of racism and social neglect in the US.

My father was concerned about what he saw was a deepening divide in American society between those who were living in economic comfort and those who were living in material deprivation, which he called "a lonely island of poverty in the midst of a vast ocean of material prosperity" in the speech. Black citizens, he noted, were disproportionately represented among the ranks of the poor, trapped in a "triple ghetto," characterized by racism, poverty and human misery.

He noted that Black workers were experiencing double the unemployment rate of white workers while earning about half their average income. He spoke about the "blasted hopes and shattered dreams" of young people who were seeking to find their places in American society, where they could lead productive lives and make their contributions to a better future for our nation.

But he understood that, while Black people were overrepresented among the impoverished citizenry, most poor people were white. He was therefore passionately committed to building a nationwide, multiracial coalition for social and economic justice. He believed that such a coalition, if trained in nonviolent social change, could transform America into a more just and prosperous nation, in which all people could enjoy the fruits of shared prosperity.

My father did not live a full year after delivering this speech, and he was assassinated on April 4, 1968. But I believe he would be disappointed in the lack of progress America has made in the nearly six decades that have passed since then.

Black workers still experience much higher rates of unemployment, and there are still large gaps in income and wealth between the races. Black citizens have experienced some positive progress toward economic and social equality, but there are reasons to be concerned about the direction of current trends.

I think he would be deeply concerned, for example, about the right-wing campaign to dismantle diversity, equity and inclusion programs, which are designed to reduce inequality, not to give any demographic group an unfair advantage. When he was assassinated less than a year after this speech, he was mobilizing the

Poor Peoples Campaign, a multiracial movement, which he emphatically stated must include impoverished and low-income whites. This group should certainly be included in DEI programs that provide education and employment benefits.

As an advocate of human rights, my father would also be very disturbed about the racially driven harassment and deportation of immigrants, with no recourse or regard for due process.

I am equally certain that he would be organizing a nonviolent movement to protect voting rights and renew the promise of democracy inherent in the Voting Rights Act of 1965. He also understood the critical importance of confronting political apathy, energizing voter enthusiasm and doing everything he could to promote a higher level of voter turnout.

Perhaps most important of all, he would be engaged in campaigns to reduce economic injustice for workers of all races. When my father was assassinated, he was engaged in supporting a labor union struggle for dignity and justice for sanitation workers in Memphis, Tennessee. He believed that union membership was a powerful antidote to economic injustice and that it was essential for economic security for workers of all races in all industries. Even today, when we talk about ending poverty and economic injustice, revitalizing the labor movement remains a central challenge we face in achieving economic security for all Americans.

When we reference the term "the Other America," we tend to think about the America we don't experience. If we are among the lucky ones living in a comfortable environment, "the Other America" means the part of our country in which a large percentage of people are living in economic deprivation. And it is disturbing that about 11 percent of Americans, or more than thirty-six million people, are today living below the poverty rate. A nonviolent movement to correct this discrepancy merits the support of all people of good will who want to end poverty and economic injustice. In addition to stronger labor unions, such a movement should include on its agenda a higher minimum wage and progressive taxation, so the poor pay less and the wealthy pay more.

But there is another way to think about "the Other America." This is the brave, new America that does not exist yet, the America of our noblest dreams, a nation where people of all races experience the benefits of peace and prosperity. This is the America of my father's "I Have a Dream" speech, in which brotherhood and sisterhood among people of different races, religions and political beliefs find room to grow and flourish. It is vitally important that we take the time to envision this America, the America that can and must be, if we are to remain faithful to the promise of equality and shared prosperity for all our citizens.

It is said that without vision, the people perish. But with this vision of unity, the people will not perish; they will thrive and prosper and create the beloved community of Martin Luther King Jr.'s dream.

"THE OTHER AMERICA" SPEECH

April 14, 1967
Stanford University
California

Members of the faculty and members of the student body of this great institution of learning; ladies and gentlemen.

Now there are several things that one could talk about before such a large, concerned, and enlightened audience. There are so many problems facing our nation and our world, that one could just take off anywhere.

But today I would like to talk mainly about the race problems since I'll have to rush right out and go to New York to talk about Vietnam tomorrow and I've been talking about it a great deal this week and weeks before that.

But I'd like to use a subject from which to speak this afternoon, the Other America. And I use this subject because there are literally two Americas.

One America is beautiful
for our situation.

And, in a sense, this America is
overflowing with the milk of prosperity
and the honey of opportunity.

This America is the habitat of
millions of people who have food
and material necessities for their
bodies; and culture and education
for their minds; and freedom and
human dignity for their spirits.

In this America, millions of people experience every day the opportunity of having life, liberty, and the pursuit of happiness in all of their dimensions. And in this America millions of young people grow up in the sunlight of opportunity.

But tragically and unfortunately, there is another America.

This other America has a daily ugliness about it that constantly transforms the ebulliency of hope into the fatigue of despair.

In this America millions of work-starved men walk the streets daily in search for jobs that do not exist.

In this America millions of people
find themselves living in
rat-infested, vermin-filled slums.

In this America people are poor by the
millions. They find themselves perishing
on a lonely island of poverty in the midst
of a vast ocean of material prosperity.

In a sense, the greatest tragedy of this other America is what it does to little children. Little children in this other America are forced to grow up with clouds of inferiority forming every day in their little mental skies.

As we look at this other America,
we see it as an arena of blasted
hopes and shattered dreams.

Many people of various backgrounds live in this other America. Some are Mexican Americans, some are Puerto Ricans, some are Indians, some happen to be from other groups. Millions of them are Appalachian whites. But probably the largest group in this other America in proportion to its size in the population is the American Negro.

The American Negro finds
himself living in a triple ghetto.
A ghetto of race, a ghetto of poverty,
a ghetto of human misery.

So what we are seeking to do in the civil
rights movement is to deal with this
problem. To deal with this problem of
the two Americas. We are seeking to
make America one nation, indivisible,
with liberty and justice for all.

Now let me say that the struggle for civil rights and the struggle to make these two Americas one America is much more difficult today than it was five or ten years ago. For about a decade or maybe twelve years, we've struggled all across the South in glorious struggles to get rid of legal, overt segregation and all of the humiliation that surrounded that system of segregation.

In a sense this was a struggle for decency; we could not go to a lunch counter in so many instances and get a hamburger or a cup of coffee.

We could not make use of public accommodations. Public transportation was segregated, and often we had to sit in the back and within transportation— transportation within cities—we often had to stand over empty seats because sections were reserved for whites only.

We did not have the right to vote in so many areas of the South.

And the struggle was to deal with these problems. And certainly they were difficult problems, they were humiliating conditions.

By the thousands we protested these conditions. We made it clear that it was ultimately more honorable to accept jail cell experiences than to accept segregation and humiliation. By the thousands students and adults decided to sit in at segregated lunch counters to protest conditions there.

When they were sitting at those lunch counters they were in reality standing up for the best in the American dream and seeking to take the whole nation back to those great wells of democracy which were dug deep by the Founding Fathers in the formulation of the Constitution and the Declaration of Independence.

Many things were gained as a result of these years of struggle.

In 1964 the Civil Rights Bill came into being after the Birmingham movement which did a great deal to subpoena the conscience of a large segment of the nation to appear before the judgment seat of morality on the whole question of civil rights. After the Selma movement in 1965 we were able to get a Voting Rights Bill.

And all of these things represented strides. But we must see that the struggle today is much more difficult. It's more difficult today because we are struggling now for genuine equality.

It's much easier to integrate a lunch counter than it is to guarantee a livable income and a good solid job. It's much easier to guarantee the right to vote than it is to guarantee the right to live in sanitary, decent housing conditions. It is much easier to integrate a public park than it is to make genuine, quality, integrated education a reality.

And so today we are struggling
for something which says we
demand genuine equality. It's not
merely a struggle against extremist
behavior toward Negroes.

And I'm convinced that many of the
very people who supported us in the
struggle in the South are not willing to
go all the way now. I came to see this
in a very difficult and painful way.

In Chicago over the last year where I've lived and worked. Some of the people who came quickly to march with us in Selma and Birmingham weren't active around Chicago.

And I came to see that so many people who supported morally and even financially what we were doing in Birmingham and Selma were really outraged against the extremist behavior of Bull Connor and Jim Clark toward Negroes, rather than believing in genuine equality for Negroes. And I think this is what we've gotta see now, and this is what makes the struggle much more difficult.

So as a result of all of this, we see many problems existing today that are growing more difficult.

It's something that is often overlooked, but Negroes generally live in worse slums today than 20 or 25 years ago. In the North schools are more segregated today than they were in 1954 when the Supreme Court's decision on desegregation was rendered.

Economically the Negro is worse off today than he was 15 and 20 years ago. And so the unemployment rate among Whites at one time was about the same as the unemployment rate among Negroes.

But today the unemployment rate among Negroes is twice that of Whites. And the average income of the Negro is today 50% less than Whites.

As we look at these problems we see them growing and developing every day. We see the fact that the Negro economically is facing a depression in his everyday life that is more staggering than the depression of the '30s.

The unemployment rate of the nation as a whole is about 4%. Statistics would say from the Labor Department that among Negroes it's about 8.4%. But these are the persons who are in the labor market, who still go to employment agencies to seek jobs, and so they can be calculated.

The statistics can be gotten because they are still somehow in the labor market. But there are hundreds of thousands of Negroes who have given up. They've lost hope. They've come to feel that life is a long and desolate corridor for them with no Exit sign, and so they no longer go to look for a job.

There are those who would estimate that these persons, who are called the Discouraged Persons, these 6 or 7% in the Negro community, that means that unemployment among Negroes may well be 16%. Among Negro youth in some of our larger urban areas it goes to 30 and 40%. And so you can see what I mean when I say that, in the Negro community, there is a major, tragic, and staggering depression that we face in our everyday lives.

Now the other thing that we've gotta come to see now that many of us didn't see too well during the last ten years—that is that racism is still alive in American society. And much more widespread than we realized.

And we must see racism for what it is.
It is a myth of the superior and the
inferior race. It is the false and tragic
notion that one particular group,
one particular race is responsible for
all of the progress, all of the insights
in the total flow of history. And the
theory that another group or another
race is totally depraved, innately
impure, and innately inferior.

In the final analysis, racism is evil because its ultimate logic is genocide.

Hitler was a sick and tragic man who carried racism to its logical conclusion. He ended up leading a nation to the point of killing about 6 million Jews.

This is the tragedy of racism because its ultimate logic is genocide.

If one says that I am not good enough to live next door to him; if one says that I am not good enough to eat at a lunch counter, or to have a good, decent job, or to go to school with him merely because of my race, he is saying consciously or unconsciously that I do not deserve to exist.

To use a philosophical analogy here, racism is not based on some empirical generalization; it is based rather on an ontological affirmation.

It is not the assertion that certain people are behind culturally or otherwise because of environmental conditions. It is the affirmation that the very being of a people is inferior. And this is the great tragedy of it.

I submit that however unpleasant it is we must honestly see and admit that racism is still deeply rooted all over America. It is still deeply rooted in the North, and it's still deeply rooted in the South.

And this leads me to say something about another discussion that we hear a great deal, and that is the so-called white backlash. I would like to honestly say to you that the white backlash is merely a new name for an old phenomenon. It's not something that just came into being because of shouts of Black Power, or because Negroes engaged in riots in Watts, for instance.

The fact is that the state of California voted a Fair Housing Bill out of existence before anybody shouted Black Power, or before anybody rioted in Watts. It may well be that shouts of Black Power and riots in Watts and the Harlems and the other areas, are the consequences of the white backlash rather than the cause of them.

What it is necessary to see is that there has never been a single solid monistic determined commitment on the part of the vast majority of white Americans on the whole question of civil rights and on the whole question of racial equality.

This is something that truth impels all men of good will to admit.

It is said on the Statue of Liberty that America is a home of exiles. It doesn't take us long to realize that America has been the home of its white exiles from Europe. But it has not evinced the same kind of maternal care and concern for its Black exiles from Africa.

It is no wonder that in one of his sorrow songs, the Negro could sing out, "*Sometimes I feel like a motherless child.*" What great estrangement, what great sense of rejection caused a people to emerge with such a metaphor as they looked over their lives.

What I'm trying to get across is that our nation has constantly taken a positive step forward on the question of racial justice and racial equality. But over and over again at the same time, it made certain backward steps. And this has been the persistence of the so-called white backlash.

In 1863 the Negro was freed from the bondage of physical slavery. But at the same time, the nation refused to give him land to make that freedom meaningful. And at that same period America was giving millions of acres of land in the West and the Midwest, which meant that America was willing to undergird its white peasants from Europe with an economic floor that would make it possible to grow and develop, and refused to give that economic floor to its Black peasants, so to speak.

This is why Frederick Douglass could say that emancipation for the Negro was freedom to hunger, freedom to the winds and rains of heaven, freedom without roofs to cover their heads. He went on to say that it was freedom without bread to eat, freedom without land to cultivate. It was freedom and famine at the same time. But it does not stop there.

In 1875 the nation passed a Civil Rights Bill and refused to enforce it. In 1964 the nation passed a weaker Civil Rights Bill and even to this day, that bill has not been totally enforced in all of its dimensions.

The nation heralded a new day
of concern for the poor, for the
poverty-stricken, for the disadvantaged.
And brought into being a Poverty
Bill and at the same time it put such
little money into the program that it
was hardly, and still remains hardly,
a good skirmish against poverty.

White politicians in suburbs talk

eloquently against open housing,

and in the same breath contend

that they are not racist.

And all of this, and all of these things tell us that America has been backlashing on the whole question of basic constitutional and God-given rights for Negroes and other disadvantaged groups for more than 300 years.

So these conditions, existence of
widespread poverty, slums, and of tragic
conditions in schools and other areas
of life, all of these things have brought
about a great deal of despair, and
a great deal of desperation.
A great deal of disappointment and even
bitterness in the Negro communities.

And today all of our cities confront huge problems. All of our cities are potentially powder kegs as a result of the continued existence of these conditions. Many in moments of anger, many in moments of deep bitterness engage in riots.

Let me say as I've always said, and I will always continue to say, that riots are socially destructive and self-defeating. I'm still convinced that nonviolence is the most potent weapon available to oppressed people in their struggle for freedom and justice. I feel that violence will only create more social problems than they will solve. That in a real sense it is impracticable for the Negro to even think of mounting a violent revolution in the United States.

So I will continue to condemn riots, and
continue to say to my brothers and sisters
that this is not the way. And continue
to affirm that there is another way.

But at the same time, it is as necessary
for me to be as vigorous in condemning
the conditions which cause persons to
feel that they must engage in riotous
activities as it is for me to condemn riots.

I think America must see that riots do not develop out of thin air. Certain conditions continue to exist in our society which must be condemned as vigorously as we condemn riots.

But in the final analysis, a riot is the language of the unheard. And what is it that America has failed to hear?

It has failed to hear that the plight of the Negro poor has worsened over the last few years. It has failed to hear that the promises of freedom and justice have not been met. And it has failed to hear that large segments of white society are more concerned about tranquility and the status quo than about justice, equality, and humanity.

And so in a real sense our nation's summers of riots are caused by our nation's winters of delay. And as long as America postpones justice, we stand in the position of having these recurrences of violence and riots over and over again. Social justice and progress are the absolute guarantors of riot prevention.

Now let me go on to say that if we are to deal with all of the problems that I've talked about, and if we are to bring America to the point that we have one nation, indivisible, with liberty and justice for all, there are certain things that we must do.

The job ahead must be massive and positive. We must develop massive action programs all over the United States of America in order to deal with the problems that I have mentioned.

Now in order to develop these massive action programs we've got to get rid of one or two false notions that continue to exist in our society.

One is the notion that only time can solve the problem of racial injustice. I'm sure you've heard this idea. It is the notion almost that there is something in the very flow of time that will miraculously cure all evils. And I've heard this over and over again.

There are those, and they are often sincere people, who say to Negroes and their allies in the white community that we should slow up and just be nice and patient and continue to pray, and in a hundred or two hundred years the problem will work itself out because only time can solve the problem.

I think there is an answer to that myth. And it is that time is neutral. It can be used either constructively or destructively. And I'm absolutely convinced that the forces of ill will in our nation, the extreme rightists in our nation, have often used time much more effectively than the forces of good will.

And it may well be that we will have to repent in this generation not merely for the vitriolic words of the bad people and the violent actions of the bad people, but for the appalling silence and indifference of the good people who sit around and say, "Wait on time."

Somewhere we must come to see that social progress never rolls in on the wheels of inevitability. It comes through the tireless efforts and the persistent work of dedicated individuals. And without this hard work time itself becomes an ally of the primitive forces of social stagnation. And so we must help time, and we must realize that the time is always right to do right.

Now there's another notion that gets out, it's around everywhere. It's in the South, it's in the North, it's in California, and all over our nation. It's the notion that legislation can't solve the problem, it can't do anything in this area. And those who project this argument contend that you've got to change the heart and that you can't change the heart through legislation.

Now I would be the first one to say that there is real need for a lot of heart changing in our country, and I believe in changing the heart. I preach about it. I believe in the need for conversion in many instances, and regeneration, to use theological terms.

And I would be the first to say that if the race problem in America is to be solved, the white person must treat the Negro right, not merely because the law says it, but because it's natural, because it's right, and because the Negro is his brother.

And so I realize that if we are to have a truly integrated society, men and women will have to rise to the majestic heights of being obedient to the unenforceable.

But after saying this, let me say another thing which gives the other side, and that is that although it may be true that morality cannot be legislated, behavior can be regulated.

Even though it may be true that the law cannot change the heart, it can restrain the heartless. Even though it may be true that the law cannot make a man love me, it can restrain him from lynching me. And I think that's pretty important also.

And so while the law may not change the hearts of men, it can and it does change the habits of men. And when you begin to change the habits of men, pretty soon the attitudes will be changed; pretty soon the hearts will be changed.

And I'm convinced that we still need strong civil rights legislation. And there is a bill before Congress right now to have a national or federal Open Housing Bill. A federal law declaring discrimination in housing unconstitutional. And also a bill to make the administration of justice real all over our country.

Now nobody can doubt the need for this. Nobody can doubt the need if he thinks about the fact that since 1963 some 50 Negroes and white civil rights workers have been brutally murdered in the state of Mississippi alone, and not a single person has been convicted for these dastardly crimes. There have been some indictments but no one has been convicted. And so there is a need for a federal law dealing with the whole question of the administration of justice.

There is a need for fair housing laws all over our country. And it is tragic indeed that Congress last year allowed this bill to die. And when that bill died in Congress, a bit of democracy died, a bit of our commitment to justice died. If it happens again in this session of Congress, a greater degree of our commitment to democratic principles will die.

And I can see no more dangerous trend in our country than the constant developing of predominantly Negro central cities ringed by white suburbs. This is only inviting social disaster. And the only way this problem will be solved is by the nation taking a strong stand, and by state governments taking a strong stand against housing segregation and against discrimination in all of these areas.

Now there's another thing that I'd like to mention as I talk about the massive action program and time will not permit me to go into specific programmatic action to any great degree. But it must be realized now that the Negro cannot solve the problems by himself.

There again, there are those who always say to Negroes, *"Why don't you do something for yourself? Why don't you lift yourselves by your own bootstraps?"* And we hear this over and over again.

Now certainly there are many things that we must do for ourselves and that only we can do for ourselves. Certainly we must develop within a sense of dignity and self-respect that nobody else can give us. A sense of manhood, a sense of personhood, a sense of not being ashamed of our heritage, not being ashamed of our color.

It was wrong and tragic of the Negro ever to allow himself to be ashamed of the fact that he was Black, or ashamed of the fact that his ancestral home was Africa.

And so there is a great deal that
the Negro can do to develop self-respect.
There is a great deal that
the Negro must do and can do
to amass political and economic
power within his own community
and by using his own resources.

And so we must do certain things for ourselves but this must not negate the fact, and cause the nation to overlook the fact, that the Negro cannot solve the problem himself.

A man was on the plane with me some weeks ago and he came up to me and said, *"The problem, Dr. King, that I see with what you all are doing is that every time I see you and other Negroes, you're protesting and you aren't doing anything for yourselves."* And he went on to tell me that he was very poor at one time, and he was able to make it by doing something for himself.

"Why don't you teach your people," he said,

"to lift themselves by their own bootstraps?"

And then he went on to say other groups

faced disadvantages, the Irish, the Italian,

and he went down the line.

And I said to him that it does not help

the Negro, it only deepens his frustration,

upon feeling insensitive people to say

to him that other ethnic groups who

migrated or were immigrants to this

country less than a hundred years or

so ago, have gotten beyond him and

he came here some 344 years ago.

And I went on to remind him that
the Negro came to this country
involuntarily in chains, while others
came voluntarily. I went on to remind
him that no other racial group has
been a slave on American soil.

I went on to remind him that the
other problem we have faced over
the years is that this society placed a
stigma on the color of the Negro, on
the color of his skin because he was
Black. Doors were closed to him that
were not closed to other groups.

And I finally said to him that it's a nice thing to say to people that you oughta lift yourself by your own bootstraps, but it is a cruel jest to say to a bootless man that he oughta lift himself by his own bootstraps.

And the fact is that millions of Negroes, as a result of centuries of denial and neglect, have been left bootless. They find themselves impoverished aliens in this affluent society. And there is a great deal that the society can and must do if the Negro is to gain the economic security that he needs.

Now one of the answers, it seems to me, is a guaranteed annual income, a guaranteed minimum income for all people, and for our families of our country.

It seems to me that the civil rights movement must now begin to organize for the guaranteed annual income. Begin to organize people all over our country, and mobilize forces so that we can bring to the attention of our nation this need, and this is something which I believe will go a long, long way toward dealing with the Negro's economic problem and the economic problem which many other poor people confront in our nation.

Now I said I wasn't going to talk about Vietnam, but I can't make a speech without mentioning some of the problems that we face there because I think this war has diverted attention from civil rights. It has strengthened the forces of reaction in our country and has brought to the forefront the military-industrial complex that even President Eisenhower warned us against at one time.

And above all, it is destroying human lives. It's destroying the lives of thousands of the young promising men of our nation. It's destroying the lives of little boys and little girls in Vietnam. But one of the greatest things that this war is doing to us in civil rights is that it is allowing the Great Society to be shot down on the battlefields of Vietnam every day.

And I submit this afternoon that we can end poverty in the United States. Our nation has the resources to do it.

The National Gross Product of America will rise to the astounding figure of some $780 billion this year. We have the resources: The question is whether our nation has the will, and I submit that if we can spend $35 billion a year to fight an ill-considered war in Vietnam, and $20 billion to put a man on the moon, our nation can spend billions of dollars to put God's children on their own two feet right here on earth.

Let me say another thing that's more in the realm of the spirit I guess, that is that if we are to go on in the days ahead and make true brotherhood a reality, it is necessary for us to realize more than ever before that the destinies of the Negro and the white man are tied together.

Now there are still a lot of people who don't realize this. The racists still don't realize this. But it is a fact now that Negroes and whites are tied together, and we need each other.

The Negro needs the white man to save him from his fear. The white man needs the Negro to save him from his guilt.

We are tied together in so many ways, our language, our music, our cultural patterns, our material prosperity, and even our food are an amalgam of Black and white. And so there can be no separate Black path to power and fulfillment that does not intersect white groups.

There can be no separate white path to power and fulfillment short of social disaster. It does not recognize the need of sharing that power with Black aspirations for freedom and justice.

We must come to see now that
integration is not merely a romantic or
aesthetic something where you merely
add color to a still predominantly white
power structure. Integration must be
seen also in political terms where there
is shared power, where Black men
and white men share power together
to build a new and a great nation.

In a real sense, we are all caught in an inescapable network of mutuality, tied in a single garment of destiny.

John Donne placed it years ago in graphic terms, *"No man is an island entire of itself. Every man is a piece of the continent, a part of the main."* And he goes on toward the end to say, *"Any man's death diminishes me because I'm involved in mankind. Therefore never send to know for whom the bell tolls. It tolls for thee."*

And so we are all in the same situation: the salvation of the Negro will mean the salvation of the white man. And the destruction of life and of the ongoing progress of the Negro will be the destruction of the ongoing progress of the nation.

Now let me say finally that we have difficulties ahead but I haven't despaired. Somehow I maintain hope in spite of hope. And I've talked about the difficulties and how hard the problems will be as we tackle them.

But I want to close by saying this afternoon that I still have faith in the future. And I still believe that these problems can be solved.

And so I will not join anyone who will say that we still can't develop a coalition of conscience.

I realize and understand the discontent and the agony and the disappointment and even the bitterness of those who feel that whites in America cannot be trusted. And I would be the first to say that there are all too many who are still guided by the racist ethos.

And I am still convinced that there are still many white persons of good will. And I'm happy to say that I see them every day in the student generation who cherish democratic principles and justice above principle, and who will stick with the cause of justice and the cause of civil rights and the cause of peace throughout the days ahead.

And so I refuse to despair.

I think we're gonna achieve our freedom because however much America strays away from the ideals of justice, the goal of America is freedom. Abused and scorned though we may be, our destiny is tied up in the destiny of America.

Before the pilgrim fathers landed at Plymouth we were here. Before Jefferson etched across the pages of history the majestic words of the Declaration of Independence, we were here. Before the beautiful words of "The Star Spangled Banner" were written, we were here.

For more than two centuries, our forebearers labored here without wages. They made cotton king. They built the homes of their masters in the midst of the most humiliating and oppressive conditions. And yet out of a bottomless vitality, they continued to grow and develop.

And I say that if the inexpressible cruelties of slavery couldn't stop us, the opposition that we now face, including the so-called white backlash, will surely fail. We're gonna win our freedom because both the sacred heritage of our nation and the eternal will of the Almighty God are embodied in our echoing demands.

And so I can still sing

"We Shall Overcome."

We shall overcome because the arc of the moral universe is long but it bends toward Justice. We shall overcome because Carlyle is right, "*No lie can live forever.*" We shall overcome because William Cullen Bryant is right, "*Truth crushed to earth will rise again.*" We shall overcome because James Russell Lowell is right, "*Truth forever on the scaffold, Wrong forever on the throne—Yet that scaffold sways the future.*"

With this faith, we will be able to hew out of the mountain of despair a stone of hope. With this faith, we will be able to transform the jangling discourse of our nation into a beautiful symphony of brotherhood. With this faith, we will be able to speed up the day when all of God's children, Black men and white men, Jews and Gentiles, Protestants and Catholics, will be able to join hands and live together as brothers and sisters, all over this great nation.

That will be a great day,
that will be a great tomorrow.

In the words of the Scripture, to speak symbolically, that will be the day when the morning stars will sing together and the sons of God will shout for joy.

About Dr. Martin Luther King Jr.

Dr. Martin Luther King Jr. (1929–1968), preacher, civil rights leader, and recipient of the Nobel Peace Prize, inspired and sustained the struggle for freedom, interracial brotherhood, and social justice through his philosophy and strategies of nonviolence.

About Martin Luther King III

Martin Luther King III is the oldest son of Dr. Martin Luther King Jr. and Mrs. Coretta Scott King.